Emotions Run Deep

Monique Renee Trotter

BALBOA.PRESS
A DIVISION OF HAY HOUSE

Balboa Press books may be ordered through booksellers or by contacting:

Balboa Press
A Division of Hay House
1663 Liberty Drive
Bloomington, IN 47403
www.balboapress.com
844-682-1282

Print information available on the last page.

ISBN: 979-8-7652-2558-5 (sc)
ISBN: 979-8-7652-2559-2 (e)

Balboa Press rev. date: 02/22/2022

Contents

Unresolved Issues

You are a masterpiece
I can't believe it myself
You are a castle made of dreams
The art of a creative soul
Seems to soar beyond expectations
Yet I'm a complete idiot
My eyes are bigger than my heart
You have no idea
How easily I fall from grace
If only we lived in a fairy tale
With a happily ever after
You are the leading man in my life
I don't want to lose you
Deeper in the ocean
I feel I'm drowning
Please save me, save me please
My strength can only carry me so far
Without you
There is no gentle touch of a paintbrush
Without you
My world is empty and bare
I promise I will see with only my heart
Instead of my eyes
And our song shall continue playing
And the sun shall rise again
Regardless of how things are right now
I know you still love me.

Please Don't Be In Love With Someone Else

In a state of solitary confinement
The passion is more intense
I love you like Jesus loves Sunday
For you are my morning prayer
It's easy to get caught up in the moment
Especially when there's nothing else to do
I can't see the sun
I may never be free
There are no signs of improvement
If only I could hear your voice
Instead of my own thoughts
It's way too dark in here
My shadow doesn't exist
This place is impossible to escape
Yet I can taste the cold air so bittersweet
Somewhere out there in the world
You stand high and mighty
With a pretty girl on your arm
But do you know who she is
Behind the painted mask?
Oh the eyes of fate
See more than what needs to be seen
My love for you is beyond
The realest of real
It's the only thing that does exist in this place
Oh please love me again
I'm sorry
I'm so so sorry
Get me out of this place
Before I lose my mind completely.

Ed Nigma

Behold,
The words to your soul are quite revealing
Heaven has finally taken me to a place of leisure
The mystery unfolds
As the clouds begin to disappear
I'm lost in a silence that is golden
My actions can't speak out loud
For if my actions speak now
My vision of you may never come true
So I remain silent in the midst of the magic
The words to your soul
Tell a story beyond belief
I see myself lingering beside you
A man of many truths
May you appear to be my new inspiration
I'm falling for you immensely
And we just met by chance,
A chance of a lifetime
A stroke of genius that is you and what you create
With a mind of a great composer
You dance your way into my heart
I am honored to be in your presence
Fireworks burst out of the sky
Indeed my actions have spoken
As well as the mystery that lies in Ed Nigma
Mesmerizing yet beautifully passionate
Your imagination soars above the stratosphere.

Love Love Love

You're in my life
Whether you like it or not
Someday you'll come back to me
When the seas are clear
When the mountains are high
When your heart decides to beat again
For this isn't the first time you left me
Staring at the moon
Wishing upon a star
I'm not one to judge the powers of the universe
All I can do is rely on faith and determination
This is love,
This is real love
I can feel it dancing in my bones
And the miracle of love
Is accepting it for what it truly is
Complicated yet undefined
Just like you
I think that's why I'm still attracted to you,
You have the heart of a ghost
And the soul of a grown boy
Let me fill you with constant pleasure
Let me fill that empty space between your ears
I think you know what I'm talking about
Hugs and kisses
Kisses and hugs
I love you.

A New Day

Your heart can race against my heart anytime
Reach out to me
As if I am still in a dream
I am not a wounded bird
I am just a lonely girl
Waiting for you to come home to me
I've got love on my mind
And I want you all over me
Your rhythm
Your rhyme
Your poetry
Touch me
And I shall be yours forever
As a new day emerges
We've built a pretty strong bond
One that may be impossible to break
You make me laugh, you make me smile
You may be a ghost
But your spirit still lives
The clouds kiss the ocean
The ocean runs deep
I will always remember you
But will you always remember me?

You Know Who You Are

And after this you shall remain
In this dark hole of suspense
You are truly defiant
Let the fog rise from under me
Let love be a mystery
For passion is power
And power is passion
Touch me and I won't crumble
You have my heart on bended knee
There are not enough mirrors in the world
To capture one's true colors
That's why I'm here, I recognize your fear
A fear I once had
When I thought nobody loved me
And now I have a reason to love again
And again and again and again
Until there's no more love left in me
I feel I am able to reach you
In your time of need
Yet you deny me your heart.

Unknown

The river is wild
And the wind is free
I'm just a lonely child
Sitting under a tree
My love is lost for the millionth time
Oh my heart never fails to sigh no more
The stars and planets are out of rhyme
Oh where is heaven's door?
God bless the unknown
Looking for the sun
God bless the unknown
Looking for the one.

Distant Hearts

...Will never beat the same again
Louder and louder the waves crash into the shore
A broken fire on a wire begins to rise
With a blind eye to the sun
I don't expect anything to happen between us
Though it would be nice to make love to a perfect stranger
Between the sheets of electric passion
Well everything in my world is electric
Even my everlasting thoughts of you
Bells and horns
Triumphant bliss
Who on this earth shall be my destiny?
Distant hearts...
I wonder how far apart we really are
For a hopeless romantic such as I
Can easily be inspired by the simplest things
The sky's the limit
So I've been told
But what about the ocean
That leads to only God knows where?

Simply Divine

I've reached a climax, oh my God
This sudden burst of energy makes me feel totally alive
Inspiration is the key to anything possible
Now I'm caught up in good vibes
And I'm forever sprung
As we make love through perfect eyes
My inner genius explores every waking thought
My mind is a presence of acute certainty
A well-discovered attribute to my forbidden knowledge
You touch my heart
You touch my soul
Then my body overflows with pure insanity
You and I will be something incredibly spectacular someday
Until then
We shall continue living our lonely lives
I miss you already
And I haven't even met you yet.

Deep Shade of Purple

I want to escape into your mind
I want to know what you're thinking
Whatever it is
Your deepest and darkest secret is safe with me
Lost and unfulfilled I am
Searching, searching to find the truth
In the middle of the road I stand
Looking at the beloved sky
My destiny has not yet fallen
For my destiny may be you
In my eyes you are the perfect chance
Like a recurring dream passing through
Invisible planes, trains, and automobiles
They don't seem to be going anywhere
But I think I'm getting closer and closer to your mind
Show me a sign
Maybe a flashing light in the blink of an eye
Ah to live another day
A mystery wrapped in a deep shade of purple
I want to touch you
I want to know what you're feeling
A vast sense of inspiration creates a solid possibility
The chemistry is there
And I'm not giving up.

This is Us

You are everything that shines
Where there is glitter
There is gold
I chase away the clouds
And give you the sun
Life is just beginning
We are both mature enough
To follow the right path
We are both mature enough
To build a meaningful relationship
I am everything that shines
Where there is glitter
There is gold
You chase away the clouds
And give me the sun
Life is just beginning.

Forget Me Not

When anxiety speaks
I listen
I dread these passionate nights alone
Yet the thought of you
Gives me so much pleasure
As I write these poems
And set them free in the wind
The moon is a sleeping sun
The sky is always blue
As blue as my heart
Swimming in the deep blue sea
Not all of my dreams are exposed
Just the ones I envision the most
With you looking into my eyes
And telling me you love me
You may have left me far behind
Like a poem in the wind
Oh please forget me not
For I will never forget you
These tears I cry
And cry alone.

Forever Your Girl

No more tears of sad refrain
As I begin to dance in your presence
The rain is so distant
I can see the sun
Bright as the first day of spring
I shall honor you with a precious gift
The radiance of time
Whisper to me your undying breath
A lonely life is not so vague
A yellow rose blooms in the light
Fragrance is good for the soul
Let me fill your heart with sweet surrender
Let me echo sweet words through your ears
The castle is keen on this fine earth
The doors are wide open
And the windows are crystal clear
The winds of tomorrow become graceful birds
Soaring ever so sweetly in the air
I am forever grateful for the joys you bring
For there are so many.

Whisper

Let me be the woman you need
Basking in the glory of fame
My eyes are like fireflies
Bursting into flames
These lips of love are eager
To tell you how naughty I've been
Your fingers glide like paper planes
Lost in the heavens above
My dearest poet
My heartfelt song
May you be in my life forever
The pen is mightier than the sword
In more ways than one
Let me be a whisper in your ear.

Blue Scarlet

Breakfast in bed keeps me afloat
With flowers that breathe the perfect aura
I am dressed in your eyes
Wide open and aware
Blue scarlet lies in the middle of the floor
As the moon and the stars connect with the sun
Let's tell lies through our teeth
You make me want you
Like a wall wants space
With painted pictures that don't exist
The colors are so wild
I can't explain
Blue scarlet is constantly on my mind
With roses as pretty as the sun
The fire is so seductive
The fire is mine
The flames rise above the sky
Leading to higher obscurity
Blue scarlet be mine forever
Under the distant blue light
I want to dance with you inside these eyes
My lips are tender and bright
A kiss so dear for the world to see
You are my shining star.

Lost in the World

Tear me apart against my dying mercy
Love me like a wet diamond
Sparkling in love's forbidden desert
There is a place called heaven
Where everything makes sense
Fear has no existence because of the angels
I am a woman of circumstance
Trapped inside the life of a poet
The bluest rose has the loneliest heart
But she dares to speak her mind
I feel her presence at my feet
As tears fall upon the face of the earth
I have lost my best friend
No amount of words can heal the pain
So I stand here in the light of day
Hoping to find a valuable truth
My pen has no reason to retire
Let's struggle between the sheets that are warm
So many stories are dying to be heard
The power within me stays
If I had no one to inspire
The angels would be at war.

Profound Misery

I miss you more than I miss myself
My life is perfectly annoying
You turn me on, but in the most fragile way
Broken pieces of a devoted mirror have fallen
And the sky is no longer blue
Where are you?
I have to know
The stars begin to fade into the darkest night
We used to be so phenomenal together
Until the planets crashed and burned
Now the very thought of you is hanging on my wall
I can't break the spell
Whether or not you're around, the tides have spoken
Love is a silent film used to express the heartache
Sorrow only comes when it's raining
Dear God let it rain outside my door
I cannot take another flood
For it's much too crowded inside, too many memories.

Touch Me in the Morning

Evasive moments like this
Never seem to steer away
A cup of coffee and a cup of steam
Together we make monogamy
The sheets are nice and crisp
Between long hours and endless bliss
And I will always remember
The flowers that linger.

A Cloud Within The Shadows

The heavens are alive
With tinted windows of gold
Life is truly an art
As sparks burst in front of your doorstep
My heart is true
You have to believe me
Every part of this journey awakens
Love is a promising state of mind
It devours all living fears
For me it's the complete experience
Lost in a valid dream
I shall float on this cloud and think nothing of it
But I choose to stay on this earth with you
For you are the center of my attention
Draped in the awesomeness of you
It hurts me to think of another love
When there is no time to waste
In the dark I am free with my thoughts
In the light I am less than naughty
Because the world is so small in the hands of God
And he is bigger than all the world
So yes I have fallen for the deepest part
This journey shall last a long while
You and I must remain a secret pact
To never give up is to win
Your beauty forsakes me, a long-lasting dream
Dying to be near a rose
Oh what is a heart without a bridge to depart?
The clouds have come to speak.

Abandoned

Love be my savior tonight
For wild winds do blow
My beauty rests upon the shore
Does heaven have a name?
I am in awe of such a scene
A delicate caress
Captivating roses meet the eye
But what is more important than love?
I treasure all that is given to me
A flame in my heart
An erotic trance
Give me something I can't afford to live without
Like a starving artist with a bucket of paint
I'd like to fall handsomely in the arms of fate
Imagining the very thought of eternity
But I can't imagine the way it feels
When all is cloudy and blue.

The Madness that is Me

I am a fond girl of misery
Caught in the eyes of a tragic boy
Shattering his fate on the dance floor
I find him to be very attractive
Like a thief in the night
Cupid thinks I'm stupid
Because I wear my heart on my sleeve
And I carry a smile
That's been dead for a while
I should bite my tongue in shame
But tender thoughts must remain uncalm
His lips blow out a delicate smoke
Giving false illusion to his eyes
This tragic boy has no resistance
I am a victim of his parade
I mustn't refrain
Love is not fickle
When it comes to a zealous heart
Indeed I speak wisely
As the passion within me inflames
For the longer I keep this secret
The sooner it will unfold
Romance is raving in the stars
Ever so brightly I shine for him
Two lovers at war become one
Behold my heart's undying wish
It is as deep as the midnight sun
That bares the soul of a twisted genius.

Absolutely Brilliant

Dare I strike a nerve this evening
When all the world's a-gloom?
A pebble seems so very small
To those who can't see it
Fake people are all the same
In their own psychotic trance
I don't understand why I'm the enemy here
Let's get personal shall we?
Yes I am angry
And it's all your fault
You doubt me when you have no reason to
You shake, shatter, and destroy
Yet I am still here
You will never get the best of me
For I am absolutely brilliant
In the eyes of a brilliant man
He looks at me and he sees a diamond
For a diamond's beauty is electric.

From My Heart to Yours

To be in love at last
One's never felt a joy so vast
The world is full of fearless souls
Who strive to achieve their goals
Faith rings true to the eternal bells
And all the rainbows and wishing wells
Oh the many mysteries of the world
God bless the one who finds the lucky pot of gold
From my heart to yours
This very heart soars
The sun captures the present day
And all the other days that lead to heaven's way
I give to you in return
A warm and passionate fire's burn
Oh the eternal bells, they ring so true
Can you hear them serenading you?

She Cries

For I am she
And she is I
Happiness rings the solemn bells
As my heart grows tender
And my spirits begin to unwind
Love is my surviving savior
A warmth that shall never fail
To be loved is something quite special
A kiss of sunshine endears the embrace of life
Therefore I have found my own peace of mind
I love her
And she loves me
For I am her
And she is me
It goes on forever and ever
The sweet sound of an angel's voice
She dares not forsake me
In my wonderful world of thinking
A poet's heart never sleeps
It invigorates passion
And all other forbidden feelings,
Feelings that can't be erased
From the walls of pure insanity.

Tears of A Rose

It is the earth's hidden star
That makes life all worthwhile
The center of the universe revolves around her
As she overcomes a love that destroys most human beings
Forbidden love is a silent killer
For nobody ever talks about it,
It is swept under the rug like an unwanted secret
Rose is a star
And she knows it too
She wears a purple ballerina dress
With her heart on her sleeve
Rose is a gorgeous light defined by natural beauty
She has an honest face and honest tears
She sparkles, she shines
I see a little bit of myself standing there
Along with the other aspiring roses that lead the way
I can't remember the last time I felt so inspired
As I place the crown on her head
She smiles as if the whole world is watching
The winds are a gentle force
Behind the mirrors of glitz and glamour
Rose is just a normal girl
Who likes peanut butter and jelly sandwiches
And a good game of miniature golf
A rose is a rose that is pure and simple.

The Glory of Love

I still consider you a possibility
You're as cute as a teddy bear
With puppy dog eyes
I just want to hug you
For my own personal pleasure
My passion burns deep
My imagination runs wild
There's a place I call home
A wonderland
Full of my most precious childhood memories
With dolls, pictures, toys, and a canopy bed
Oh how the years go by
But memories are forever
I close my eyes
And I hear your voice
Telling me to come back to earth
In my heart I am a child
In my mind I am a poet
I can create a world
With just one simple thought.

Hypnotic

Beyond a dream
There is something out there
That is fragile yet innocent
Like a mystery undisguised
Look into my eyes
And get lost in them for a moment
You will fall in love with me
Let me take you beyond a dream
A place where shooting stars
Turn into delicate little doves
Yes there is a heaven within these eyes
If you can get inside my head
God only knows what is beyond heaven
The universe is made of many different worlds
With intense colors that fly
And echoes that are near and far
Let yourself live vicariously through me
I will wipe away the tears
And put a brand new smile on your face
I shall be your waking revelation
For I am a mystery undisguised
Love me until the end of time
Whatever we paint on canvas together
May lead to a statue of greatness.

Simply Marvelous

Love's final curse has brought me here
I can't seem to separate myself from the thought of you
You're a bad boy I happen to enjoy
But let's face it
This is all just a fantasy
As dreams begin and passions ignite
Your kiss enthralls me through mystic air
No matter what lies you tell
My heart still can't resist you
One thousand roses and counting
Yes we've done this before
Red, white, pink, and yellow
Secretly I'm wanting more
Maybe it's the fault in our stars
Though one can never tell
The universe is so wide open
With possibilities flying everywhere
I want to know what's on your mind
May your thoughts rain upon such curiosity
With one thousand rose petals and counting
Shower me, shower me simply marvelous.

I Love To Be In Love

I remain lost in your eyes
As the world disappears for a while
You are a burst of inspiration that never goes away
Sunny days, starry nights
A thousand bright lights in a small city
Where rainbows and unicorns collide
My imagination shall suffer the consequences
Your truth is my truth
You turn this lonely rose into a lovesick angel
Every time you speak your rhyme
I'm feeling a whole different vibe with you
If only our lips could touch
A kiss attached to a careless whisper
Has no bounds between the clouds in the sky
And the voices that carry
You know who you are
I know who I am
We are bigger than heaven above
Bigger than anything that is greater than love
I love you more than I love to be in love.

We Belong Together

I'm high on champagne
And champagne kisses
Your love is like fire
It burns me up inside
I'm chasing butterflies in my dreams
I'm feeling worthy of you
The secrets between us shall evolve
Heart to heart
Face to face
You embrace me in your presence
As the mystery connects us
We are free to speak our minds peacefully
I'm in pain
I'm going insane
In the rain
Without an umbrella
The Sunday blues remind me of you
All alone in a dark room
Waiting for the sun to shine
Well heaven is a rose
Hanging by a rose cloud
As the raindrops are slowly dripping away.

Free

My words run off the page like thoughts unlimited
I can't control my feelings
Poetry is a place where I can breathe
Along with my pen in hand
My life is simply brilliant
It is not all black and white
There is also color so rich and rare
I shall paint you a picture in a verse
I shall give you a space in my heart
Anything to make you see the beauty in me
There is nothing like a poet's dream
I dare you to dream with me
I shall whisper these words in your ear
For all the world to hear
Because I am free
And I am not afraid
To express myself entirely
The rain before the storm is always electric
I am wrapped in rose petals and untold secrets
Fall, fall upon me electric rain
I want to feel the warmth of such tears.

The Miracle of Solitude

I don't want to build a bridge between us
I am reborn, let me live again
We are all young and restless
And we don't deserve to die
Visions of blue remind me of you
The deepest part of my soul is where I belong
Soft as angels buried in the sea
I find you desperately seeking me
A sense of romantic youth has flourished
Touch me in the sky way up high
For even the prettiest things are in the sky
Simple yet faded is the love below.

Omar

The happiest love is the greatest love possible
I cherish my days and nights
When poetry speaks
I just have to write
My thoughts are always wandering
God gives me strength to endure the world
For there are many challenges to be sought
I have a muse with incredibly gifted eyes
Is there a junkyard in heaven where poets dream?
Long live the way of the weathered child
Singing songs in the wayward rain
It is I, and Omar is the sun
He is the passion that bleeds my name
A kiss upon a rose breathes fire
With a love so true I am amused.

Love is A Crazy Emotion

A little child is sleeping in the wind
Silently she aches for her mother
Who lives for the pleasure of living
But often forgets her dying name
The heart is in a fragile state of mind
The eyes are piercing to the sun
Romance is in favor of everlasting treasures
A mother and her child are flying the beloved kite
But only in a dream that doesn't exist to anyone else
Heart-shaped balloons always spark the fire
That leads to the eternal sun
Love me not for what I am
A child of a vast-less mother
So beautiful like a gypsy in the night
I long to see you there
Where everything is free to roam the earth
Everything that is magic of course
And all will be bright until the day she dies
But for now, let us live in the moment.

My Hero

You've become my best friend
The only truth that seems righteous
You are a rare diamond
You shine as you are
And I am a rare diamond
I shine as I am
There is no other love such as this
A hero's touch, a poet's bliss
The heart's flame cannot resist
As I embrace the magic that is you
Our fate may be lost
Between the stars and the sky
When I think of us together
The world is a completely different place
A river of tears ignite
Behold these eyes that are captured by the obvious
The power within you never fails
Your walls are so deep
But are they too deep
For me to climb?
Ah hero worship
Yes I've been touched by an angel
An angel from heaven.

Simply Misunderstood

I am a queen in God's eyes
But to others I am simply misunderstood
No one knows the beauty of my heart
Therefore I shall seek for a husband
And not a follower
I am longing for that one truelove
Red roses never lead me astray
I will find my greatest destiny
It won't be easy
But love is worth risking it all
There's somebody out there
Who is crazy about me
Cupid's arrow never fails
I am bound to the spirits that carry me deep
Take this halo and make it shine bright.

Hungry Like A Rose

Dreamy days and dreamy nights
Passing through this incredible storm
I am not forever young
Your love for me is dying still
Yet there's no reason to be fearful
As the clouds disappear into the unknown
The world is so silent
Yet my destiny feels inevitable to me
Inevitable I say, inevitable in every way
The road to freedom is mighty close
Life can be a lonely friend riding in the wind
I sing as if I am broken
A long and tender kiss
Is not enough to save me
This rose that cries for mercy
Shall linger in the minds of the enchanted
I love you my darling
But I am not fully awake
I sleep in the innocence of stars united
For dreams don't exist in this private room
Only thoughts that proceed with caution
Red is the color of immense desire
Trembling in the eyes of the weary
Somewhere there is a secret you despise
My heart begins to rise from the ashes
But is it beating?
Aching to find the truth
The roses in the fire are slowly burning
I will never forget you
All the flowers in the world
Can't compare to our pretty love.

Emotional Blackmail

Open your eyes to this insipid rose
Let me tell you fact from fiction
Why erase the sky
When the sky is innocent?
Every word is immense through obvious pressure
For this is a very special poem
Through God's grace I have written such entirety
The feeling of wanting another man is no longer at risk
It is my pride that fails me
Therefore I shall be alone
What dire expense shall lead to such misery?
The rose falls from truth
As I shy away from life's prospects
I abandon myself in vain
Oh the missing element has not yet been found
The pieces of the past are hiding
And I will always love you
As long as you're on my mind.

This is for The Glory

As long as my heart is with you
I'm forever content
I may not know your name
But I know your face
Breathing beside me like a broken star
Lost in the rain and forever mine
For darkness is the cure for light
As I touch you from afar
My truelove speaks of angry yearning
Drowned by doves and violins
I am not at liberty to challenge you at war
The wildness that makes me human
The love that I feel for you
Please do not validate me with your presence
For if you do
You'll never forgive yourself
The whole point of being a star is to shine bright
We are like cupids in the rain
Finding each other
Don't ever underestimate me
For I am your queen
Reigning before you in your very dreams
Oh how gorgeous am I?
Heaven and earth couldn't be more loving
As I touch my heart
And you touch yours
What will be the mystery of this crime?

Beauty and The Beast

To my innocence I must be fair
The eyes that kiss my face begin to linger
The sweet smell of love in the sky
Way, way up high
Is the man who fears me
An airplane begins to crumble
At least my heart is falling
I touch a blank existence
I breathe a vast resilience
The windows leave a certain fog,
A fog that is not mistaken
I tell my lies through restlessness
And sleep demands the truth
What is this love that beckons me?
I long to evoke a feeling
That hairy beast is oh-so neat
Its presence is the presence of a king
So dark and full of rage
Bursting out of a cage
The thunder becomes birds of prey
Salvaging the evening sun
As windows break between the shores of fate
I dare not see tomorrow
At last love's soft hands tickle my feet
I shall pray upon defeat.

The Bells

The miracle of heaven is the loveliest illusion
I think happy thoughts of you
Attached to the rose petals that fill my head
Warm kisses caress the inevitable
My darling shade of blue
Sometimes the seasons change for good
As the chapel of love remains
With this ring I be wed to you
The most darling of all praises
Love me tenderly through all the years
And I will gladly ignite the bells
Freedom rings for the flowers across the street
There is no other youth like ours
The lost letters between us
The absence of time
A large heart has so much to provide
As my imagination wanders about
Quietly you give me chills
I am not guilty of loving such a man
For such a man is you
And this is only Sunday
My favorite day of the week
Forgive me for all the voices I can't contain
There is so much joy in one's laughter
But only to keep them safe
And the bells weaken like little lambs
Romantic is the sky
So high upon your praise

Together we will find our missing destiny
Lost in such a raging sound.
Oh the bells, the bells are calling
I want the ink to unfold
You shall be my company for a while
Here is the key to my door...

Angels

An antique glimmer up in the silver sky
Soaring through the clouds so high
Showering me with uniqueness across the world
Coming to unity as the miracle wings fold
The earth spins beautifully around her atmosphere
The sweet enigma unsolved is near
Drawing me into the illusional adventure in her eyes
My intense heart glides upon our treasuring goodbyes
Her beauty is uplifting
The glow is heavenly
I love the way her magic sings
She twirls so peacefully
She slowly fades away to the pearly gates
My overwhelming tears are gently falling down a river of praying
fates
I secretly avow my promise to her for an endless friendship
I'm taken away by the extraordinary spell she casted upon my
fingertip
Her beauty is uplifting
The glow is heavenly
I love the way her magic sings
She twirls so peacefully
Stars floating in my mind
Sailing to capture her cloud I hope to find
My distance remains a secret untold
Her magnificent imagery she gives me to hold.

Fearless

I'm not afraid of the unknown
Yet I'm as sweet as a chocolate truffle
Wrapped in the hands of bliss
You have me at hello
Every time you speak
For you're the unknown
Watching over me
Yes my conscience weighs a ton
Forgive me for my restless style
Love is not a consolation prize
It's a gift
As we dream up the perfect life together
Without falling too fast
Yet we shall fall on our own
When the time is crazy
And out of this world
Friends can be lovers
And lovers can be friends
Let's turn off the lights
And hear Cupid scream.
If I were a brilliant poet
I'd write my brilliant words
On your brilliant lips
Then I'd kiss those brilliant lips
For all brilliant eternity.

Untamed

Poetry fills me like the dawning air
I write with a simple pen
Between the sheets the words are so deep
I am dying to escape more
Let us feel
Let us breathe
Let us recognize our mental state
My woes grow weary
And my heart sings the blues
Only because I am in love with an impossible idea
There is a bright side to every story
In the land of make-believe.

Bashful

Heaven hear me now
The crooked seas are wicked
The greater the force
The greater the reward
I want to spend the night at your house
Where dreams have their own meaning
And the stars reach out to the sky
I am alone in every room
A picture of the moon is brighter than him
And I wonder where my truelove lies
For the bottom of the sea has gone
I am a vicious sting at the end of the day
Tie me to a tree
But don't rescue me
Let him find me in despair
I shall wait patiently while the Tin Man grows
My heart melts for the hero involved
Kiss me desperately in your presence
Until the night begins to fold
Oh heaven hear me now
Chivalry is not quite dead
Somewhere there is a poet in disguise
Aching for the words to come out.

Who Am I Living For?

I'm thankful heaven can be found
Upon the hills so very high
The doves that fly away become more brilliant
The eyes of solitude do shine
In the midst of Thanksgiving
I roam for a gentle holiday
One that can spare my troubles
Let there be peace on earth
I want more than just a simple greeting
I wish all the best of luck
To the towns that are seeming
I hope they find their identity under the sun
Well my hope for everything seems valuable
I can't risk a forbidden love
Can I steal a good lover without any haste?
I am thankful the sky is blue
My home is where my heart resides.

Let's Bang The Drum Slowly

Your love is like kryptonite
And I know this is wrong
But I'm feeling you right now
Touch my body and I'm yours
Kiss these lips
And we shall make a revolution
As the drum follows the beat of my heart
For we are within the spirit of the moment
You and I
In a band of our own
May your sweet love give me pleasure for all eternity
In life and death
There is only one rule,
To be and forever be
So let's bang the drum slowly
I shall give you my total being
And if a rose shall never die
Then we shall let it be.

A Rose Within A Dream

With the wind beneath love's sailing boat
I treasure you honestly
My darling fate will never be replaced
And this I am sure of
For you are my heart's repeating joy
I just want you to know
My feelings of great pleasure
A beautiful marriage that's inside my head
As we both cherish the love we pursue
The darkness is so romantic
I can see the stars
My faithfulness gently falls from the ashes
To wake, my love, is a simple thing
But to dream is not so simple
For the world is so loud within a crowd
Oh be with me till sunset darling
Then the wind will blow my way
I can picture the moon
Bringing a rose to shore
She is as beautiful as a dying bride
I must be with her
I must praise
The very thought of you inside this rose
As the wind captures your eternal beauty
You are so beautiful
And apparently divine
Behold what is a promising farewell
Oh dream, dream a little dream of a rose
So precious and astounding to me.

About the Author

Monique Renee Trotter was born in Citrus Heights, California. She hopes to reach people with her deepest revelations, innermost thoughts, and greatest hopes. Writing poetry is her passion, and she has three other books out as well: A Mindful Awakening, My Poetry Speaks, and Killing Me Softly with a Poet's Song. Monique definitely wants her voice to be heard. She also loves to read poetry. Her favorite poets are Sylvia Plath, Maya Angelou, and William Shakespeare. Poetry is music to her ears.

Printed in the United States
by Baker & Taylor Publisher Services